Geoffrey's Journey Home

A Story About One Dog's Journey Home to Heaven and How I Learned to Live Without Him

by
Pamela Barnett

AuthorHouse™
1663 Liberty Drive, Suite 200
Bloomington, IN 47403
www.authorhouse.com
Phone: 1-800-839-8640

AuthorHouse™ UK Ltd.
500 Avebury Boulevard
Central Milton Keynes, MK9 2BE
www.authorhouse.co.uk
Phone: 08001974150

First published by AuthorHouse 2/7/2006

ISBN: 1-4259-0828-4

Library of Congress Control Number: 2005911339

Printed in the United States of America
Bloomington, Indiana

This book is printed on acid-free paper.

Bloomington, IN   Milton Keynes, UK

authorHOUSE

Acknowledgements

I would like to thank God for leading me on my life's journey and for sending me all the special people who helped me write this book. I would also like to thank all the Poodle Pampering customers for sharing their loving pet stories with me.

I would also like to thank my husband for having the patience to live with all the dogs and for supporting and comforting me as they all make their journey home.

2000
Christopher Laura Geoffrey
Zana Ladd Gracie

4th of July 1996
Christopher Geoffrey Gracie
Zana Ladd

Geoffrey Gracie Christopher
Laura Ladd Zana

Geoffrey Ladd Gracie Zana Christopher

Ladd Christopher Geoffrey Gracie Zana

Gracie Christopher Zana Geoffrey
Laura Ladd

Gracie Laura Christopher Geoffrey Zana
Ladd

December 2004
Geoffrey and Zana
4-20-92 — 2-22-05

Vic, Pam and
The Barnett Gang

Zana, Christopher, Gracie, Laura, Geoffrey
Christmas 2003

Silent Night
HOLY NIGHT
2002

MERRY CHRISTMAS FROM
POODLE PAMPERING

2002
Christopher and Laura
6-15-89   5-9-91
11-7-03   5-13-05

Prologue

I was born in January 1961. Ever since I could remember, I loved dogs. A little black poodle was the first dog I met; I still remember him. When I was three, I played with my Grandma's dog Heidi (a German Shepherd Dog). I think knowing Heidi led me not only to work with dogs, but to teach others about them as well.

Prince - Cocker Spaniel
1981-1994

I have spent my life searching for pet shops, lost dogs, puppies-for- sale, and any place where I could pet dogs.

I also got involved in training them. I've trained dogs since 1981 when I joined Tail Waggers DTC (Dog Training Club) in Chicago. I loved it …I won titles in obedience and in herding.   At that time, I owned a Cocker Spaniel, and I knew he needed to be groomed. I soon discovered a small grooming shop called Poodle Pampering on the north side of Chicago. One day I asked Marge, the owner, if she needed any help. She asked, "What can you do?" Didn't she know I spent my life loving dogs? "I could do anything!" I thought. My first day bathing dogs was so hard. Sure, anyone can bath one dog that knows you, but try bathing 25 dogs that only want to run away! Later, I was given the opportunity to learn grooming. I was scared at first, but with a lot of hard work, I managed to master my skills. I've been grooming since 1988. I then bought Poodle Pampering from Marge in 1993.

I have spent everyday since then doing the best job someone could ever pray for. This truly is my life's mission. One day, Shirley, a co-worker at the shop, asked if I wanted a puppy. Shirley was raising Shelties, and her dog Crystal just had a litter. My first Sheltie Christopher was a blue merle. By 1995, I owned six Shelties: Christopher, Gracie, Zana, Laura, Geoffrey, and Ladd. Grooming, training, and showing dogs became my life.

Pam with shelties
1996

Now that I've been grooming for 17 years, I've decided there had to be something I could give back to dog lovers everywhere. I prayed for guidance for about a year, but I truly did not know what that "something" was going to be.

In 1995, I experienced the sudden death of my mother. After her death, I wanted to share my experience with others to try helping them deal with this kind of pain.

I felt that I had to write a book about dying, but I really didn't like to write at all! Well, I still had to do something to help people who were afraid to die. I felt my true gift of faith would see me through this desire.

Years went by, but I never stopped thinking about writing a book. Then the veil was lifted from my eyes, and I knew the book would be about a dog's journey home, rather than, a person's journey. What better subject to write about? The book would combine my experience with dogs, my faith, and the inspiration to help people.

Unfortunately, I did not see the light until the week our youngest dog Geoffrey was dying. I truly lived through every grieving moment recorded in this book, and I believe I went through the grief and pain so I could write it from my heart. After Geoffrey died, I knew I was going to write this book. No one knew about this but God and me. A week after Geoffrey died, my friend Susan gave me a gift. I opened it and it was a blue leather- bound journal with 'Geoffrey's Journey' imprinted on it. I knew then, that this was going to be the beginning of a new chapter in my life and a healing process for me to get through the loss of Geoffrey.

I hope this book brings you comfort for your loss. There will always be a prayer for your dog and you in my heart.

I'll see you too… at the Rainbow Bridge.

God Bless,
Pam Barnett

Laura Zana Ladd Gracie Christopher Geoffrey

Picture of Me, Mom and a Black Poodle
The first dog I ever met. Summer of 1962

Geoffrey

GEOFFREY'S JOURNEY HOME

This book is dedicated to all the owners who cry endlessly for their dogs. May you find comfort in the knowledge that you will be together again someday.

Let's journey together to help ourselves get through the sadness of losing our best friends. Only true "dog" people can understand the real pain associated with that loss.

What is it about the loss of a dog that can bring a man or woman to his or her knees in grief?

Only unconditional love.

Table of Contents

Chapter One
BONDING WITH A DOG

Have you ever really loved a dog? If the answer to this question is "yes," then you are not alone. Millions of people from all walks of life: rich, poor, blind, handicapped, young, and old alike have not only loved dogs but have gone through the joy of having and the pain of losing more than one dog in their lives.

We say we are not going to get "attached" to our dogs, and then a few days later we wouldn't give them up for anything. We bond with them so quickly because they depend on us for everything. They follow us everywhere. How can we not bond with something that gives us undivided attention, not to mention, unconditional love?

Once the bond has been established we stay home more, or we find places to go with our dogs. This is why we end up hanging around with other "dog" people. We all have the same thing in common. We get involved with all kinds of activities with our dogs, or we just hang out at home and watch T.V. together. We never feel alone.

Those who have "human" children (I say this because people who don't have children call their dogs their "children") still consider their dogs' part of the family and would not part with them.

People from all walks of life have the same thing in common. They are so attached to their dogs they don't know how they would ever live without them. How are you going to live without your dog? What is it that builds this bond?

Geoffrey

Geoffrey and Laura
2003
Laura 5-9-91   5-13-05

Geoffrey
1st Place
9 mos. old

Geoffrey
4 mos. old

Chapter Two
WHY DO WE "LOVE" DOGS?

"Love," by far, is the most powerful word ever. You can experience it and you can give it. Why do we pour out all of our love for a dog?

In the 17 years I've worked with dogs and their humans, I have found one thing in common. People truly, unconditionally, love their dogs. They love them because their dogs are always there for them; dogs never hurt their feelings. Dogs are always happy to see their humans, and they never leave them. This sounds exactly what every human searches for in his/her life, doesn't it? I believe this is why we give our love to dogs. Dogs are very unselfish, never asking for anything in return.

One day I saw a dog tied up to a grocery cart full of junk, and moments later a homeless man, very dirty, walking slowly, headed toward the cart. Suddenly, the dog started wagging his tail and jumping up and down. What I saw was unconditional love. I'm sure that homeless man felt very rich just because of that dog.

Dogs are not only our companions, they can save us physically as well. There are dogs that go out of their way to rescue humans. These dogs think on their own, and most of the time risks their own lives to save our lives. Here are a couple of true stories taken from the television program <u>Animal Miracles</u>.

"Chelsea and the Gunmen"[1]

A peaceful evening in the suburbs is shattered when two armed men attempt to rob a couple. But their golden retriever isn't about to stand by and let her loved ones get hurt. She puts her own life on the line and is seriously wounded in the process. She's courageously protected her owners and prevented the robbery. She did survive.

"Hand Me the Bat"[2]

A truck driver is in the midst of hauling a load of electronic in a tractor-trailer with his Rottweiler Mariah by his side. He pulls over at a truck stop for a quick bite of lunch, but instead finds himself the target of a couple of robbers. As he attempts to deal with the thugs, a third robber is sneaking up behind him, armed with a baseball bet. Outnumbered, he doesn't stand a chance on his own. Then suddenly Mariah comes to his aid, leaping seven feet out of the truck's passenger window to save the man she loves.

I have customers who go out of their way to take care of their dogs. Some have taken out loans to pay for medical expenses. One senior I know will not have knee replacement surgery because she does not want to leave her dog. Another who has cancer says she can't die because she has to take care of her dog.

Love is what makes all of us do the things we do for our dogs. Most of us would go out of our way and possibly risk our own lives for a dog before we would ever do so for another human being.

Love never fails.

Geoffrey
4th of July

Geoffrey 1995

Geoffrey
3 mos. old

Geoffrey 1997

Chapter Three
GEOFFREY'S STORY

I was in search of a Bi-Blue Shetland Sheepdog with a blue eye. This is where Geoffrey's story begins. In October of 1993, I was searching for a replacement of a Bi-Blue Sheltie with a blue eye that I lost due to kidney failure at five months old. Seven months later, I found one.

In the summer of 1994, my sister Christine and I took a journey to a breeder in a small town in Iowa. There were puppies everywhere. I narrowed down the search by picking out all the Bi-Blue ones. Then I narrowed the search even more by choosing the only blue-eyed dog. I chose "Geoffrey," naming him after the giraffe from the Toys 'R Us commercials, and that became his registered name.

For the six-hour drive home, Geoffrey would not stay in his cage. Christine ended up holding him the entire way so he would not cry.

Geoffrey actually turned out to be a very mature puppy. He never played with toys. His only desire and motivation was food. He grew up to be super obedient, but he also had a mind of his own. Geoffrey did the funniest things. He was the joy of my family – that is, a family with five other Shelties. He was also the most dominant male I had. I broke up fights over food daily between Geoffrey and the other dogs.

Cameo Victoria Secret
5-20-93   10-4-93

In 2000 I married my long time friend Vic. The dogs and I had to adapt quickly to a whole new way of living. No longer was Geoffrey sleeping next to me on the pillow. Geoffrey's role changed, but he still did everything with me. I also saw him doing other things that he thought of all by himself.

His favorite trick or stunt was putting his paws up on the counter and laying his head there, waiting for someone to see him and give him a cookie. He would wait there no matter how long it would take. You see, waiting for food was Geoffrey's favorite thing to do. He was so patient, and he could sniff out the tiniest piece of food from any corner. Another one of his trademarks was staring. And all he would do was lay there and stare at the food. When human friends would come over, they were amazed at how he would lay his head on the table, waiting for something. He would even stare at the cabinet where the treats were housed. As long as someone had food, Geoffrey was a friend.

Geoffrey staring at a cookie
July 2004

Geoffrey's head caught in screen door

We would also get a big kick out of the way Geoffrey would walk up the stairs very slowly and with one leg at a time. He never hopped up the stairs like other dogs. When we would let him out we had to open both the front and screen doors, and the screen door did not close quickly. Geoffrey would hurry out, turn around, and put his head in between both doors, where he would stay until we let him inside. If I tried to push his head out with my foot, he would bite it.

Geoffrey

The last funny thing Geoffrey did involved one of those rubber toys that you can put treats in; "Well, I thought, "Finally, the perfect toy for Geoffrey." This would be one he could work on for awhile to get his treat-reward. I stuck three cookies in the toy and gave it to him. I left him on the couch while I worked at my grooming table nearby. A little while later I went to see if he got the cookies out. To my surprise, I found that he had not touched the toy at all! He just lay beside it. I should have known better. I ended up digging the cookies back out and giving them to him. Was he too smart or was he too slow? I tried the "towel trick" with Geoffrey, the one in which you put a towel over the dog's head and see how long it takes him/her to remove it. The quicker the dog removes it, the smarter he/she is. Well, Geoffrey never removed it; I eventually had to remove it myself!

Geoffrey with toilet paper

Geoffrey could also be aggressive, but in a protective way. He would go after anyone who came near our car; he would bark at everyone he saw, including the customers. I always thought he would protect me. For 10 years I was not afraid of driving or being in the shop alone, because if he was with me I could always depend on him to ward off, or at least scare anyone by his pouncing off the door, and his constant, uncontrollable barking. He had teeth bigger than any dog I knew, which is not your typical Sheltie characteristic.

Geoffrey was so close to me for so long. I could even hear him "blink" his eyes. He stared at me with those gorgeous blue eyes for 10 years. No human or dog had ever given me that kind of attention.

In June 2004, Vic, Geoffrey and I, along with our other Shelties, Gracie and Laura, rented a cabin in Michigan. We had the best time. Geoffrey loved running around, but he was too scared to walk out on the dock. He really wasn't the outdoorsy type. He'd rather stay with me in the kitchen while I was cooking. I didn't know it at the time, but that trip would be our last. I couldn't have asked for a better summer with Geoffrey.

Geoffrey at Little Smokey Lake, Michigan, June 2004

The next month, July 13th, to be exact, it was a warm, sunny, and beautiful day. The dogs and I were working at my grooming shop alone that day. I let everyone out in the backyard to relieve themselves, and for some reason I went out with them. Gracie was waiting at the back door while Geoffrey was walking towards the door. As I watched him, he just started to stagger, hit the building, and collapsed under Gracie. I scooped him up and ran in the shop. He seemed fine; I think picking him up that quickly probably started his heart again. Thinking back, he exhibited the same behavior at home in the backyard in 1999. At the time I was behind Geoffrey, and I thought he just stumbled, but it seemed to be the same collapse as this recent one.

Geoffrey at Little Smokey Lake, Michigan, June 2004

Geoffrey at Little Smokey Lake, Michigan, June 2004

When I put him down he seemed perfectly fine, so I didn't think anything of it. That was a Tuesday. The next week he started acting very strange, like he was dizzy or in pain. I took him to the vet and he did a blood test. The blood test came back with nucleated red blood cells, which indicated that there was a serious problem. Geoffrey's red blood cells were not normal; oxygen was not being carried through his body normally. Something was destroying them.

The next step was to do an x-ray and an ultra-sound. At this point Geoffrey just wasn't himself. The x-rays did not show anything significant, but the ultra-sound showed a nodule in his spleen and a one-inch tumor in his liver. The vet said there was no bleeding, but I still didn't know why he fainted. I asked him to do an echocardiogram of his heart. Again, this test showed Geoffrey was fine. I had hoped it was a heart problem, because my vet was a heart specialist and he would most likely be able to fix it. I asked for a diagnosis, and he said that it was an autoimmune problem; Geoffrey's body was attacking itself for some reason. There was nothing we could do.

Almost a month went by, and Geoffrey was not in any pain and eating just fine. I decided to do nothing, but wait and see what would happen. I almost thought everything was all right, but then on Sunday, August 22nd, Geoffrey was very quiet. He ate his breakfast but just laid around. After church, my husband and I went to his company picnic. We didn't return until 4:00 pm. By then, Geoffrey was a little bloated and his gums were pale. I decided to see if he would eat – he did, no problem. He was fine as long as food was involved. Open the cookie jar and he would come running! However, other than eat, he would just lie around. I did not take him to the vet because there was nothing they could do, and he did seem okay. If he was still like this on Monday I would take him in.

I was now thinking Geoffrey had cancer--maybe that tumor in his liver was cancerous. This type would be a fast-spreading cancer. Our other dog Christopher died of liver cancer on November 3rd, 2003. Experience taught me that if this is what Geoffrey had, it was going to be a very quick and painless death. He would just bleed internally, get weaker and weaker quickly, and finally die.

However, I was still hoping this illness wasn't a reality either. That Sunday night I really didn't think he was going to make it, so I stayed up with him, watching him and lying with him as he slept. If he was going to die I wanted to be there so he would not have to die alone. To my surprise, Monday morning came and he seemed to improve. We all went to work, but on the way home at the end of the day, Geoffrey started acting very strangely; he couldn't get comfortable in the front seat where he always sat.

I dropped the other dogs off at home and took him to our south side vet. She listened to his heart and said he has an arrhythmia. She let me listen, and for a moment I was relieved that it was his heart and that we had just happened to catch it in time. She wanted to do an x-ray. When she came back with the x-ray and put it up against the lights, it showed a lot of whiteness. She said there was no definition, meaning that Geoffrey's cavity was full of freestanding blood. She showed me the syringe full of blood that she aspirated from his abdomen. I was so devastated; I didn't know what to say. She graciously said her dog died of the same thing, and just before she put her to sleep, she gave her dog a great last meal. I asked her what I should do. She said I could either put him to sleep then or take him home, give him whatever he wanted to eat, and just be with him. I had our other dog Laura with us, and I went out to the car to go home. I loaded the dogs in the car with Geoffrey in the front and Laura in the back. I had food in the car and wanted to see if Geoffrey would eat. If he wasn't going to eat, then I knew he was not feeling well and would have put him to sleep right away. As I was feeding Geoffrey, Laura suddenly started vomiting, probably as a reaction to her shots, and the fact that she is 13 years old. I rushed her back inside and the doctor gave her Benedryl. I called my husband, who was on his way to the Cubs game. I told him the sad news, and he turned around and came home. When I was back in the vet's office, I asked her how long she thought Geoffrey had – she said less than a week.

This was the beginning of the end for our Geoffrey.

How was I going to say good-bye?

Geoffrey's last picture
August 2004

Me and Geoffrey

Chapter Four
HOW TO SAY GOOD-BYE

When I started working on what would be this chapter, it had been six weeks since we lost Geoffrey. Geoffrey was given a week to live. How hard is it, knowing you are going to lose your dog within such a short time frame?

Since he was given a week to live, that meant I wanted to spend every moment with him. I was very fortunate because Geoffrey could go to work with me. That Tuesday we decided if Geoffrey wasn't any better we were going to put him to sleep. I made the appointment for 6:00 pm on Tuesday, August 24th, 2004. All day I would look at him and stop to kiss him. He got lots of cookies. As the day flew by as it always did, I tortured myself by saying silently, "Geoffrey only has five hours to live. Geoffrey has only four hours to live." Believe me, whatever you are faced with when his/her time comes, you will know it. Trust me and don't count his/her time down. It just worsens the pain.

At 3:00 pm I finished work and my friend Susan and I were sitting next to Geoffrey. He just looked at us. He didn't look like he was going to die. I looked at him and I said, "Geoffrey, do you want to stay another night?" I thought he nodded his head,

"Yes." A moment later Susan said, "Did you see that? He nodded, "'Yes.'" When she said that, I felt relieved, because I knew I saw the nod too. By now it was about 4:00 pm and I decided to call and cancel his journey home for now. I felt so much better. Geoffrey was making a remarkable comeback. I didn't know what it meant but I knew one thing for sure, I was never going to plan his death again. I had to practice what I preached. I told Geoffrey, "You're going to have to make decisions yourself. You can just give up when you can no longer go on."

I continued to feed him all the treats he ever hoped for. I knew when he refused food his time was near. Geoffrey and I spent the rest of the week together, day and night. I even continued sleeping on the couch with him. I wanted to be there just in case God called him home in the night.

Friday, August 27, 2004, was our final workday together, and it was a great day. One of my customers from my south side shop called, wanting to find a home for her friend's miniature poodle. I told her I had the perfect people in mind. I called my north side customers up and asked them if they would like the poodle. They both said, "Yes." Unfortunately, now I was faced with getting the poodle to them. He was going to be dropped off at our house around 7:00 pm. My other customers were 25 miles north of me. It was Friday, and the last thing I wanted to do was to drive up north. I changed my attitude though, because I felt I was being selfish. I also didn't want to drop the dog off on Saturday, our day off.

My customers, who were waiting for this new love of their lives, were very excited. I thought that Geoffrey and I would bring them their new addition. That day, wouldn't you know it, there was something going on at Soldier Field – traffic was terrible. However, I stopped worrying and felt peaceful because if this was Geoffrey's last night on Earth, we were going to spend it doing something truly worthwhile. The people we were going to see were some of Geoffrey's favorite people. The wife didn't even know he was sick until I told her. When we got there it was love at first sight for the poodle; his new Dad held him. Meanwhile, Peggy went over to say good-bye to Geoffrey. A lot of tears were shed, both of joy and of sadness.

We got home about 9:30 pm. We decided to go to bed. It was another stormy night with lots of lightning and thunder. I could see Geoffrey's silhouette when the sky would light up: he was up a lot, and he seemed uncomfortable. He would look at me and I would lie next to him. I fell back to sleep and I awoke at 5:30 am. Geoffrey was not on lying on the couch, and I was praying that I wouldn't find him lying on the floor, dead. I found him standing in the hall staring at the floor. I knew, without a doubt, the end was here.

I had a whole week to say good-bye and what a great week it was. I was truly blessed. I believe saying good-bye to a pet is more meaningful when we care for and love them, whether we're with them for a long time or for a short while. Then, when the end inevitably comes, we know we gave them the best lives they could have ever had. Just keep telling them that we'll see them again.

Chapter Five
WHEN THE END COMES

By far, this was the hardest chapter to write, because I had to relive a lot of the sadness as I was writing it. What do we do when we know the end has come? I never planned what I would do, I didn't even think about it. I still really didn't believe he would die.

At 5:30 am I saw him standing there, staring at the floor. I scooped him up in my arms and carried him outside to see if he would go to the bathroom. He was able to stand and do his business, although he was very slow. Once he got moving, it seemed his blood was pumping some energy in him. I hurried inside to feed our other dogs. I knew he would not be able to eat and honestly, I didn't want to see him ever refuse food. Remember, eating and staring were his favorite things to do. It would have hurt me to see him not be able to eat.

When I went back outside I couldn't find him at first, but then my eyes adjusted and I saw the full moon was shining on him. He was just walking in a circle. It was so sad to see him that way. I picked him up, lifted him high, and looked up to heaven saying, "Father, into your hands I commend his spirit." I don't even know what made me say that.

I brought Geoffrey back in the house and laid him on the couch. I woke my husband up and told him Geoffrey was dying. For the next two and a half hours Vic and I just watched Geoffrey slowly fade away. Though his breathing was very labored, he seemed so peaceful. As we were waiting for him to take his last breath, Vic and I would speak ever so softly to each other. At one point Geoffrey just lifted his head up and looked right at Vic. We looked at each other and decided he still wasn't ready to go. We discussed when to take him to the vet. We knew the only thing they could do was put him to sleep. We wanted to wait as long as we could because Geoffrey seemed so peaceful. We were trying to be quiet because he was falling asleep, and we did not want to wake him. We were actually hoping he just wouldn't wake up.

At about 8:00 am Vic quietly said, "Do you think we should go?" I said, "Okay, let's go." From a sound sleep, Geoffrey raised his head and looked at the both of us. What came into my mind was his look, as if he were saying, "Hey, I'm trying to die and you want to go somewhere?" Remember, even though they seem to be "out of it", they can still hear you.

Since he was awake, we decided to leave for the vet who was 40 miles away. Vic carried him out and we brought Gracie, his favorite companion, with us. I wanted her to see him dead so she would know what happened to him. I laid with him on the floor in the back of the minivan. I remember the song lyrics that were playing when Vic turned the car on: "Thank you, thank you, thank God for you, the wind beneath my wings." It was the song Bette Midler sang in the film *Beaches*. I cried for the next 40 miles.

When we got to the vet's I went in to see if they were ready for us. This gave Vic time to be with Geoffrey. When I returned to the van, Vic was lying with Geoffrey. I leaned in to help Geoffrey up, he stood, but he collapsed. Vic carried him in his arms and I followed. About ten feet from the door Vic just lost it, and I thought he was going to collapse. He and I just stood there sobbing like the end of the world had come. There were two ladies getting into the car where we were standing and they started crying too. The next thing I remember was being in the room with Dr J. and his son. I was holding Geoffrey's head in my hands. Geoffrey had the blank stare – gone were his blue eyes. I'm not sure if he was gone before Dr. J. gave him the blue shot. I remember him saying, "I don't know if I can find a vein." I asked the Blessed Mother to help him. He eventually found one. Geoffrey's heart stopped and Dr. J said, "He's gone." I could not believe it. I was devastated. Vic and I said good-bye again. I just wanted to pick Geoffrey up and hold him. I still wish I had done that.

Finally, it was over. Our Geoffrey had gone to heaven on the Feast Day of St. Augustine, just before 9:00 am on August 28, 2004.

Vic brought Gracie in to say good-bye to her playmate of ten years. She just sniffed him and turned her head. I think she had already sensed he was dying.

A rose sent in sympathy.

Chapter Six
HOW TO LET GO

The 40-mile ride home was so long and so silent. Now came the replay of the entire ordeal. Over and over I went through every moment. How was I going to accept this and learn to go on?

No matter how long we have our dogs or how long it's been since we lost our dogs, some of us learn to let go and some can never let go. Letting go takes patience. We need to realize the end is always the beginning of something new.

It had been about six weeks since my last written entry. I've gone over and over in my head, how to let go. It was January 2005 then and Geoffrey had been gone four months. Sometimes it felt like yesterday and sometimes it felt like it happened so long ago. The one thing I have learned about letting go is not to let go...completely. Always remember the joy you felt when you were together. You can always hold onto your memories. Forgive other people who don't understand.

You will know time is healing you when a day goes by and you haven't even thought of your old friend, not because you don't miss him/her, but because you're re-emerging to take care of your life and the lives of other loved ones.

When you finally reach the point of missing them so much and feeling so lonely, then it may be time to think about another "friend." Believe me, when you open your heart to the possibility of getting another dog, it is also then that the healing continues.

Chapter Seven
HOW TO GET THROUGH THE PAIN

This chapter was also a difficult one to write. I was still not sure at that point, how to get through the pain. I had to experience the tragedy firsthand before I could help others.

In November 2004, I had the opportunity to get a small 6-pound 14-month-old Maltese. How meaningful – Geoffrey loved small white dogs. I talked it over with my husband and thought very hard about getting a new dog. We really weren't sure what we would do with a 6-pound dog! Vic finally agreed to the idea. Olive, as we called her, was the medicine I needed to help me heal. She needed care and I needed to take care of another dog.

On December 10, 2004 we picked up a six-week old lab puppy. He truly was the final dose of medicine we needed. Now I spend my days constantly taking care of the two new ones. I contrast them to Geoffrey because Geoffrey was never as mischievous as these young ones are! Coincidentally, Olive and Rhett (the lab) play together just like Gracie and Geoffrey played ten years ago.

Give love another chance…please.

Olive

Olive

Rhett and Olive

Rhett 4 wks

Rhett 6wks old

Rhett 3 mos.

Rhett

Rhett and Olive 2005

Chapter Eight
MY SPIRITUAL INSIGHT INTO "WHY"

Rhett and Olive

Why does God send us dogs to love? He knows how attached we are going to get. He knows how hurt we are going to feel if and when something happens to them. Why do you think we have dogs? I'll tell you what I've always believed.

God sends us dogs to teach us *unconditional love.* He wants us to learn from them. Dogs can be everything from our eyes, to our hands, to our ears, to our legs. They can even talk for us if we are confused or are in trouble. They are our companions in good times and in bad. They love us and are willing to die for us. They grieve for us and miss us when we are gone.

What other friend can you cry your eyes out with and then receive consoling kisses? When you are at your lowest you go to them for comfort. Child or adult, we all would do anything for our dogs. Even prisoners are comforted and calmed when they have dogs to train. God has a plan with dogs; I think he wants us to love people like we love our dogs.   Could you love another human being like you love your dog?

I also believe God wants us to be totally forgiving, much like our dogs. Can you imagine the Lord loving you more than you love your dog? God never lets anyone be satisfied with anything short of Himself. The only other greater love given to us is Jesus.

This prayer is often quoted: "Lord, please help me be the person my dog thinks I am. Help me to love like you love, more and more every day."

Here are other scriptural verses that are inspirational:

"But now ask the beast to teach you, and the birds of the air to tell you: or the reptiles on earth to instruct you, and the fish of the sea to inform you. Which of all these does not know that the hand of God has done this? In His hand is the soul of every living thing, and the life breath of all mankind."

Job 12: 7-10

"Let everything that has breath give praise to the Lord."

Psalm 150:6

Other Tools to Help You

1. Keep a journal of your dog's life & his/her death. Writing is great therapy.

2. Cut off some hair or fur and save it by putting it in an envelope. In about six months, take it out and shape it into a heart. Put your dog's collar and heart-shaped hair in a shadow box.

3. After your dog is cremated, obtain his/her ashes and keep them in a special urn.

4. Always, always remember that God, not human beings, make the final decision when it's time for friends to go, not us. Erase the "guilt" and the phrase, "If I only..." from your heart.

God, please choose my next "best friend" for me.

Geoffrey's Ashes
4-4-94   8-28-04

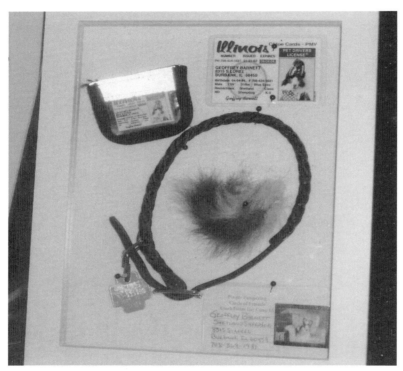

Geoffrey's collar, hair, ID in shadow box

Chapter Nine
STARTING OVER: A NEW CHAPTER

I did not think Vic and I would be starting over so soon with two new dogs. You will know when it's your time to start over – search your heart – pray about it, ask for your heart's desire. Our lives are always about starting something new. Sometimes I still wish things were back to the way they were, but Olive and Rhett have truly brought laughter into our home again. Before this book was sent to the publisher, we added a German Shepherd Dog puppy named Noah to our family.

God bless all of you who have taken the time to read this book.

Pam, Noah 3 weeks old

Pam, Rhett, Noah 8 weeks

Rhett and Noah

Rhett vacation 2005 August

Rhett

Rhett summer 2005

Noah 10 weeks old

Rhett with a pheasant
November 2005

Noah in leaves

Christmas 2005
Rhett, Olive, Gracie, Noah

Chapter Ten
TESTIMONIALS FROM OTHERS

Our Katie died March 8, 2002. She was 14½ years old. She had many different illnesses and surgeries during her life, but she would always bounce back quickly. She was a strong little girl. Dave would say to her every morning: "You are my pretty, perky, Katie- cutie. You're my summer- lower-morning- star- puppy. You're the fairest of 10,000 little Lhasa Apso puppies in the whole world, my little angel puppy."

She became very ill at the end and during the night had a stroke. Shortly after, she passed away in her sleep at the vet's office. After the doctor called us, we went in to see her. She was wrapped in a pink blanket. She was so pretty. I talked to her, kissed her, and held her, crying my eyes out.

Then we went home and our kids visited us and made us dinner. We had many phone calls from friends. I had to take a few days off from work. During that time I went to Barnes & Noble and bought books on pets and dying. I also put all of Katie's pictures in an album. I felt like I was on a mission.

We received her ashes and I made a little altar on our table in the kitchen with a beautiful angel statue standing behind her ashes. I also put her pictures, along with fresh flowers and candles on the table. I did this for many, many months. It brought me a little peace. I never wanted to come home after work anymore, though we had Charlie, our Cocker Spaniel. He couldn't take Katie's place.

Through all this I did a lot of praying. I know now that Katie will be waiting for me when I get to heaven. We brought Annie home nine months later, another Lhasa Apso, of course.

By Pat Macfarlin

ඔ

"No louder shrieks to pitying heaven are cast
When …dogs breathe their last."

Only one who has sincerely loved a dog can understand these words of Alexander Pope.

January 30th was a cold day so I allowed Jackson, my beloved, aging Shih Tzu to use the piddle pads I kept for him. He bounded out of bed, did his duty and was ready for a small breakfast. I was excited because the next day, January 31, would be his 13th birthday.

When Jackson first came to live with my husband Ernie and me, I told him he had to live to at least 20 years old, as I would be an old lady then and would have to spend less time without him. I had met some of Jackson's breed that was 18 and 19 and still walking the neighborhood, so I felt I was not being foolish.

Jackson's life had not been without difficulty as he suffered from many illnesses and had had seven operations. While others wondered why we kept spending the money, to us he was worth every penny. He loved and was loved in return.

Now after surviving <u>almost</u> 13 years, even though Jackson was deaf and blind, I believed we had a shot at that 20-year goal. He was happy, in no pain, and getting regular medical attention.

It was late afternoon, going into evening, when Jackson began to act strangely. He would not put his head down, he was panting for no discernible reason and would not look at me. I tried to give him water but he refused. I sat next to him reading and watching. About 10 pm he started throwing up foam, but it worried me, as this was somewhat unusual. I called the emergency clinic, answered their questions, and waited while they checked the chart he had with them. Jackson had been there several times.

The vet I spoke with said if he continued to vomit I should bring him in. My husband arrived home at midnight and I told him what was wrong and that I was taking him into the clinic. Ernie knew we had been through this drill many times and Jackson had always come home happy and feeling better. Since Ernie had worked for 10 hours, I told him to get some sleep and I would be right back.

At the emergency clinic, the veterinarian looked at Jackson, listened again to my recitation of the facts, and told me my darling Jackson had a fever of 106. She said they would keep him overnight and start an IV.

A feeling of horrible dread came over me. Yes, I had been through this many times, and after telling Jackson he had to fight, he came home happy and feeling much better. While waiting for a technician to come and get him, I held him tight. He was still panting and would not put his head down. I hugged him and said, "I know I always ask you to fight so you will get better. But you have been through so very much. I will understand if this time you want to rest."

It killed me to say that and it was with a heavy heart I left for home and a night of sleeplessness.

At 6:30 AM, January 31st, I got a call to pick up Jackson and to take him to our regular veterinarian. I changed clothes quickly, running to the car; elated he would be all right. I started for the clinic. Just five minutes after seven I ran in the door and said I was there to pick up Jackson. I was told, "Go into Room 4 and the doctor will talk to you."

Suddenly the day did not seem so bright. Usually they brought him out, I paid the bill and we left with the doctor's report and any x-rays.

In Room 4 I sat, tense and anxious, until the door opened and in came the vet – without my Jackson. She told me as gently as possible that just before 7:00 am Jackson had a seizure. All efforts to help him were in vain. My heart had died at 7:00am, exactly 13 years to the minute from the day he was born. My baby would not be coming home.

I left in shock, carrying his last x-ray and last vet report. I drove around for two hours before I could wake my husband with the horrible news. I didn't cry – maybe it was shock.

After waking Ernie, I called a very few close friends to tell them. Then I cried my heart out. They came with flowers, hugs and cards. It was no easier. That night I slept out of sheer emotional exhaustion.

I had never dreamed of animals of any kind and had never dreamed in color – at least in the dreams that I remembered. That night I dreamed of a huge yard with beautiful green grass, hundreds of colorful flowers, a picket fence – and dozens of dogs of every breed. They were playing and having a good time with no humans in sight.

Then a voice said, "Don't be too sad. I'm where I'm supposed to be and I'm feeling great. I can see and hear and play."

I woke up sobbing. When I told Ernie he said, "You were so much a part of each other's heart that he had to make sure you would feel better." I knew I had married a beautiful man who loved Jackson just as much as I did.

The healing was slowly beginning. The crying did not stop, especially when I had to see his toys and bed. Good friends helped by remembering all the funny little things he would do. A month passed but I could still not stand to see a dog walking down the street. I couldn't even summon pats for the beautiful dog, Jake, who lives next door.

It is just shy of one year. I cry as I'm writing this because it seems like it just happened today. There is one big difference. My new companion is upset over the tears. He is kissing them from my face.

After four months of slowly getting back to normal I realized it was entirely too quiet in the house. I took long walks but they were lonely ones. I decided it was time to look for another pet to love and care for. After many phone calls and a trip to another state, I came home with Teddy. He is a Shih Tzu but one I got from a reputable breeder this time. He is a different color and has his own quirky personality. But I love him deeply and Ernie has come to accept a new smiling face.

I believe Jackson is waiting at the Rainbow Bridge to greet me when the time is right. In the meantime, I will care for his little "brother" and remember the wonderful times past – and look forward to the wonderful times still to come.

By Luella Leu

ଔ

Katie

Katie Memorial

Jackson

DUPER By Jan Casella

I feel in my heart
He was God's special gift
Sent at a time
When I needed a lift

I was losing faith
Unable to conceive
When along came Duper
To help me believe

I loved this dog
Like no other
So my son got a pup
Instead of a brother

It was no secret
This love affair
Nothing could split
The spirit we shared

If you're lucky, they say
It will come once in your life
As for me it just ended
It cut like a knife

I have so many memories
That will help my heart mend
I'm the luckiest person
To have had such a good friend

Duper

I love you Duper

In Loving Memory
'Gracie'

Christmas 2005
9-15-90   1-7-06

Geoffrey's Best Friend

We prayed that God would let her make it to her 15th birthday and she did. She was doing great. So we prayed that she would be with us for another Christmas and she was. The day after the Epiphany, also known as the 12th day of Christmas, Gracie made her journey home to heaven. I wish I could have been there to see Geoffrey and Gracie meet again. Thank you God for letting us have her for the full 12 days of Christmas. A Christmas we'll never forget.

December 2005
Noah   Rhett
4mos   1yr

January 2006
Noah   Rhett   Olive
5 mos   1yr   2yrs

This is the beginning of the new chapter in our lives, with our new dog family.

Epilogue

I was truly inspired to write this book. This book was written entirely in the Adoration Chapel at St. Bede's Catholic Church in Chicago.

My life-changing moment occurred when I was holding Geoffrey's head as he was starting his journey home. As he was dying before my eyes, I was inconsolable. At that instant I thought of Jesus in Mary's arms after he died, and for the first time I felt how real Mary's pain was. I know it sounds crazy, but I believe I was given a special gift that day. I hope this book comforts and inspires you to live your life to the fullest and be thankful for every moment.

I have lived through every chapter of this book; without these experiences, this book could not have been written.

This book is dedicated to all the dogs that have left "paw prints" on our hearts.

Thank you, Geoffrey for 10 years of unconditional love.

See you at the "Rainbow Bridge"

The rainbow is God's covenant; remember how you feel when you see a rainbow.

I will establish the covenant with you, that never again shall all bodily creatures be destroyed by the waters of a flood; there shall not be another flood to devastate the earth. God added: "This is the sign that I am giving for all ages to come, of the covenant between me and you and every living creature with you: I set my bow in the clouds to serve as a sign of the covenant between me and the earth.
--GENESIS 9: 11-13

Just this side of Heaven is a place called
The Rainbow Bridge

When an animal dies that has been especially close to someone here, that pet goes to Rainbow Bridge. There are meadows and hills for all of our special friends so they can run and play together. There is plenty of food and water and sunshine, and our friends are warm and comfortable. All the animals that had been ill and old are restored to health and vigor; those who were hurt or maimed are made whole and strong again, just as we remembered them in our dreams of days and times gone by.

The animals are happy and content, except for one small thing; they miss someone very special to them, who had to be left behind...

They all run and play together, but the day comes when one suddenly stops and looks into the distance. The bright eyes are intent; the eager body quivers. Suddenly he begins to break away from the group, flying over the green grass, his legs carrying him faster and faster. YOU have been spotted, and when you and your special friend finally meet, you cling together in joyous reunion, never to be parted again. The happy kisses rain upon your face; your hands again caress the beloved head, and you look once more into the trusting eyes of your pet, so long gone from your life but never absent from your heart. Then you cross Rainbow Bridge together...

--Anonymous